The following book is going to introduce you to basic concepts in investing/trading on the financial markets. It is best suited for readers with no prior formal financial education. If you have some background in finance, you can still read on, because the post can serve you as a quick summary to refresh your financial markets knowledge.

If you reached this page, most probably you have decided to start investing or trading on the financial markets but are not sure where to start. Here are some of the topics that are frequently asked about by other people who are starting, just like you. Take a look and see that you are not alone in this journey.

Let's start!

contents

1.What Is A Market?

The word market itself has many uses, but most commonly people use it to refer to a place where commercial deals are concluded. This can be a physical market as in "I went to the market to pick up some fresh tomatoes" or a general like "the housing market is slowing down" or the "the stock market is going strong" etc.

In your daily life you are always participating in one market or another because you are constantly making deals and financial transactions. These can range from trivial things like buying groceries and filling up your tank with gas to bigger ones like buying a house or investing your savings in stocks.

Similarly, the financial markets are a place where people gather to make deals with financial instruments. According to the types of products traded, the financial markets are divided into stock markets (also known as equity markets), commodity markets, derivative markets, currency markets, etc.

The marketplace where you trade stocks is known as a stock exchange or stock market. You've probably heard of at least one of the major stock exchanges in the world:

New York Stock Exchange, based in New York City, United States

NASDAQ, based in New York City, United States

London Stock Exchange, based in London, United Kingdom

Deutsche Börse, based in Frankfurt, Germany

Japan Exchange Group, based in Tokyo, Japan

Korea Exchange, based in Seoul & Busan, South Korea

Hong Kong Stock Exchange, based in Hong Kong, Hong Kong

The commodity market is a financial market where commodities are traded. Of course, the commodities are not physically exchanged on the market. Instead the deals happen with futures contracts. There are "soft" commodities such as cocoa, soybeans, and sugar and "hard" commodities (usually mined) such as gold, copper, and oil. The most popular commodities and futures exchanges are the Chicago Board of Trade (CBOT) and Chicago Mercantile Exchange (CME) which merged into the world's largest futures exchange market – CME Group.

Another very popular financial market is the foreign exchange market, also known as FX market, Forex market, or currency market. This is a global marketplace where national currencies are exchanged against one another. For example, Euros are exchanged for US dollars, or British pounds to Japanese yen. In contrast to the equity and futures markets where the trading is centralized in an exchange, the forex market is decentralized and is traded over-the-counter (also known as OTC).

The traditional markets have been around for quite some time now. Commodity and currency trading and exchange have been around since ancient times. The modern foreign exchange, stock, and commodity markets emerged around the 1600s. A breakthrough in the financial markets was the adoption of electronic trading which started in the 1970s.

Now you have an idea of what is a market and particularly what is a financial market. You also learned a little bit about the world stock, commodity and futures exchanges, and the foreign exchange market.

Let's go forward to the next question.

2.How Can I Trade On The Markets?

There are various ways in which you can access the markets. Generally, it depends on which asset class you have decided to trade.

How Can I Trade On The Stock/Futures/Forex Market?

In order to trade on the traditional financial markets, you would need to open an account with a broker.

4.What Is A Broker?

A broker is a financial institution that allows you to connect to a market or an exchange to place your trades. As an intermediary the broker charges you a fee in the form of a commission or a bid-ask spread. Brokers are usually supervised by a regulator according to the jurisdiction they reside to protect their client's assets.

Here are some important things to consider when you are looking for a broker to open your trading account.

5.Trading Costs – Commission Or Bid-Ask Spread

One of the first things to look at when deciding where to open your trading account are the brokerage conditions. The different brokers charge different commissions or offer different bid-ask spread.

6.What Is A Broker Commission?

A broker commission is a type of fee paid to a broker for handling financial transactions on a trader's behalf. As we mentioned earlier individual traders cannot trade directly on an exchange. Instead they use the service of a broker who acts as an intermediary between the client and the exchange. The commission is the compensation which the broker receives for this service. The commission can vary in size and the way it is applied. Usually it is in the form of a predefined fee. It can be charged by deal (flat fee, regardless of the volume traded per deal), per stock or futures contract traded (x amount per stock or contract) or as a percentage of the notional value of the deal.

7.What Is The Bid-Ask Spread?

The bid-ask spread is the difference between the bid price and the ask price of a security. The bid-ask spread is typically the price of liquidity. Liquid markets have lower bid-ask spreads (thus they are cheaper to trade), while the spread in illiquid markets can be significant. I addition to the market spread some brokers add markup as an alternative to charging a broker commission. This way all the costs for the client are included in the spread.

8.Trading Tools

Nowadays most brokers provide web-based or desktop executable trading platforms. Some of them have also mobile applications or can be accessed by APIs. The most popular trading platforms for Forex trading that are not associated with a particular broker are MetaTrader 4 and MetaTrader 5. For stocks and futures trading the popularity prize goes to Trade Station and Ninja Trader. A lot of brokers have their own in-house build multi-asset trading platforms where you can trade almost every popular instrument – currency pairs, options, stocks, ETFs, futures contracts, etc.

Good stuff! You now know the basics about the markets and what are the ways you can access them. We have briefly mentioned the different types of products you can trade. It is now time to learn more about each one of them.

9.Financial Instruments

There is a huge variety of financial instruments to choose from when you decide to start trading. In the next few paragraphs we are going to go over the most popular ones.

10.Stocks

Stocks or also known as shares or equities are most probably the most popular investment vehicle int the world. Almost everyone has heard about the stock market or at least has seen a movie about Wallstreet and is familiar that people can profit from trading stocks. But what exactly happens when you buy a stock?

A stock is a form of security that represents proportionate ownership of a company. When you purchase a stock, you receive a share of the equity. If the company is privately held, the equity deals are arranged directly between the parties. When a company wants to attract additional capital, it can decide to go public. This means that it should undergo an IPO (a process of Initial Public Offering) and if it is successful its shares can be listed for trading on an exchange. Once this is successful, the shares become available to the general public for trading. The market where the IPO happens is known as the primary market. The market where normal trading activity happens is known as the secondary market.

11.Derivatives

A derivative is commonly described as a financial instrument that derives its value from another security. This other security is referred to as an underlying asset. The underlying asset can be any other financial instrument: a stock, commodity, currency, etc. Below is a list of the most common derivatives:

12.Forward Contracts

Forwards are the simplest derivatives. A forward contract is a deal in which the buyer and seller enter a contract to exchange the underlying asset for cash on a specific price and on a specific date in the future. The price, the quantity, and the future date at which the transaction happens is decided on the day of the deal.

The parameters of the deal are agreed upon by the buyer and the seller without any intervention from a third party. This means that forward contracts are traded over-the-counter (also known as the OTC market).

The essence of the forward transaction is that the buyer is obligated to buy the underlying asset, while the seller is obligated to sell it on the agreed date and price.

13.Futures

Futures are very similar to forward contracts. What is different is that futures contracts are standardized. This means that the quantity, the date of the transaction (known as the expiry date), etc. are determined not by the buyer and the seller, but by a third party – the exchange. As a result, the buyer and seller of a futures contract can focus on the trading activity while the exchange is responsible for the additional aspects of the deal.

Futures contracts are classified based on their underlying assets. For example, the futures on stocks are called stock futures. Respectively other popular futures contracts are classified as commodity futures, index futures, and currency futures.

14.Options

Options are another variety of a deal that arranges a transaction on a later date. An option is a contract in which the buyer buys the possibility to purchase or sell the underlying asset on or before a specified date in the future but doesn't have the obligation to do so. At the same time the seller is obligated to buy or sell the underlying if the buyer decides to exercise his option. The buyer pays compensation to the seller for this choice, which is called option premium. If the buyer of the option contract decides not to exercise the option, the deal with the underlying asset doesn't occur, but the seller keeps the premium.

Similar to futures contracts, options are also classified according to their underlying assets – commodity options, index options, stock options, currency options, etc.

15.Contract For Difference (CFD)

A contract for difference, popularly known as a CFD is a derivative popular mostly in Europe which allows the traders to profit from price deviations of the price of the underlying asset without owning it.

In a contract for difference the two parties – the buyer and the seller take the current price of the underlying asset as a reference and make a deal without transferring ownership of the underlying asset. In case the price goes up, the seller agrees to pay the difference to the buyer (the buyer gains), and respectively if the price goes down the buyer agrees to pay the difference to the seller (the seller gains).

CFDs originally emerged in London in the 1990s as a type of equity swap. They were initially used mainly by hedge funds and institutional traders. They became very popular because they were traded on margin and were a cost-effective way to gain exposure to stocks on the London Stock Exchange, without having physical holdings. Later, CFDs were introduced to retail traders and became very popular because of the easy access and the possibility to trade on margin.

CFDs emerged as an instrument to swap single stocks but have proven to be a very effective way to gain diversified exposure to the stock market by trading a whole index instead of picking individual stocks. Right now, the most traded contracts for difference are Index CFDs, followed by commodity CFDs and single stock CFDs.

16.Financial Spread Bet

A spread bet is a derivative that is available to retail traders only in the United Kingdom. It is working the same way as a contract for difference, with the additional benefit that the profits realized in spread bets are exempt from capital gains tax.

17.Exchange-Traded Fund (ETF)

An Exchange-Traded Fund (ETF) is another popular exchange-traded security. An ETF is an alternative investment vehicle that is traded like a stock that tries to replicate a market index. It consists of a basket of securities based on an index. The basket can consist of stocks, commodities, or even bonds. For example the SPDR S&P 500 ETF (known as SPY) is an ETF that tracks the S&P 500 Index and the SPDR Gold Trust ETF (known as GLD) is an ETF which tracks the price of Gold. What is specific to ETFs is that the fund has actual holdings of the assets which it is set to track. For example, the SPY has holdings of the stocks that are constituents of the S&P 500 index and the GLD has holdings of physical gold. This means that when you buy an ETF you are actually getting hold of a fraction of the underlying assets.

WOW! That is quite a lot of instruments. What's next?

18.What Is An Index?

An index is an indicator that is used to track the changes in the stock market. It is derived from the prices of a basket of stocks traded on an exchange. Usually these are the most liquid and actively traded stocks for the exchange. Any change in the prices of the stocks included in the index results in a change of the value of the index.

Indices are used by investors as a summary of the market movements. They can also be used as benchmarks for comparing the performance between different markets or sectors. Major indices are a good indicator you can check when you want to see how the market is doing. The most popular ones are:

Dow Jones Industrial Average (^DJI) – popularly known as Dow Jones or simply the Dow. This is a stock market index that measures the performance of the top 30 companies by market capitalization that are listed on the stock exchanges in the United States.

S&P 500 Index (^INX) – also known as the S&P or SP500 is another major US index. It measures the performance of the largest 500 publicly traded companies, listed on exchanges in the United States. It is one of the most followed equity indices, because it is considered to give the best representation of the US stock market.

Nasdaq Composite (^IXIC) – popularly referred to as the NASDAQ or NAS100. This is a stock market index of the stocks listed on the Nasdaq stock exchange. The composition of this index is heavily weighted towards information technology companies.

DAX Performance index (^DAX) – this is a stock market index that consists of the 30 major publicly traded companies that are traded on the Frankfurt Stock Exchange in Germany. It is commonly referred to as the DAX or DAX30.

FTSE 100 Index (^UKX) – the Financial Times Stock Exchange 100 index, also known as FTSE 100 and formally called "the Footsie" is the major stock index in the United Kingdom. It consists of the 100 companies with the highest market capitalization that are listed on the London Stock Exchange.

Nikkei 225 (^NI225) – the Nikkei 225, also known as just the Nikkei or the Nikkei Stock Average is the stock market index which represents the performance of the top 225 companies that are traded on the Tokyo stock exchange.

19.Stock Market Indices Specifics

Indices are generally not tradeable. However, as you already know there are ETFs and derivatives such as CFDs and futures contracts that are based on indices that you can use easily to replicate the performance of the index.

Stock market indices are constructed through a price-weighted or market-capitalization-weighted approach. A price-weighted approach assigns more weights in the index to the stocks with a higher price. An example of an index constructed using this way is the Dow Jones Industrial Average.

The weight of each stock in a market capitalization-weighted index is assigned according to its market capitalization. An example of such an index is the S&P 500, where the large companies like Apple and Microsoft have significant weight in the index, while the stocks with smaller market capitalization contribute less to the changes of the index.

20.What Are The Different Types Of Markets?

Markets can be classified based on various factors. For example, what is the type of the transaction, which types of instruments are traded, etc.

21.Over-The-Counter (OTC) Vs Exchange Trading

The type of transaction depends on the way it is conducted. Transactions can happen over-the-counter (OTC) or on a centralized regulated marketplace (Exchange).

OTC transactions happen directly between two market participants without any centralized intermediary. OTC markets are decentralized and unregulated. Forex is the biggest OTC market.

Exchange-traded transactions are conducted on regulated marketplaces. These transactions happen on a centralized physical system according to the rules of the exchange. Exchanges provide a range of facilities that let the operations run smoothly. These vary from standardizing the way different instruments are traded to clearing the deals between the buyers and the sellers. The various entities submit their orders to the exchange where they are recorded in a common book. As a result, there is increased transparency about the transactions. Stock exchanges are a typical example of a regulated marketplace.

22.Markets According To The Type Of Instruments Traded

The second market classification is based on the type of instruments traded.

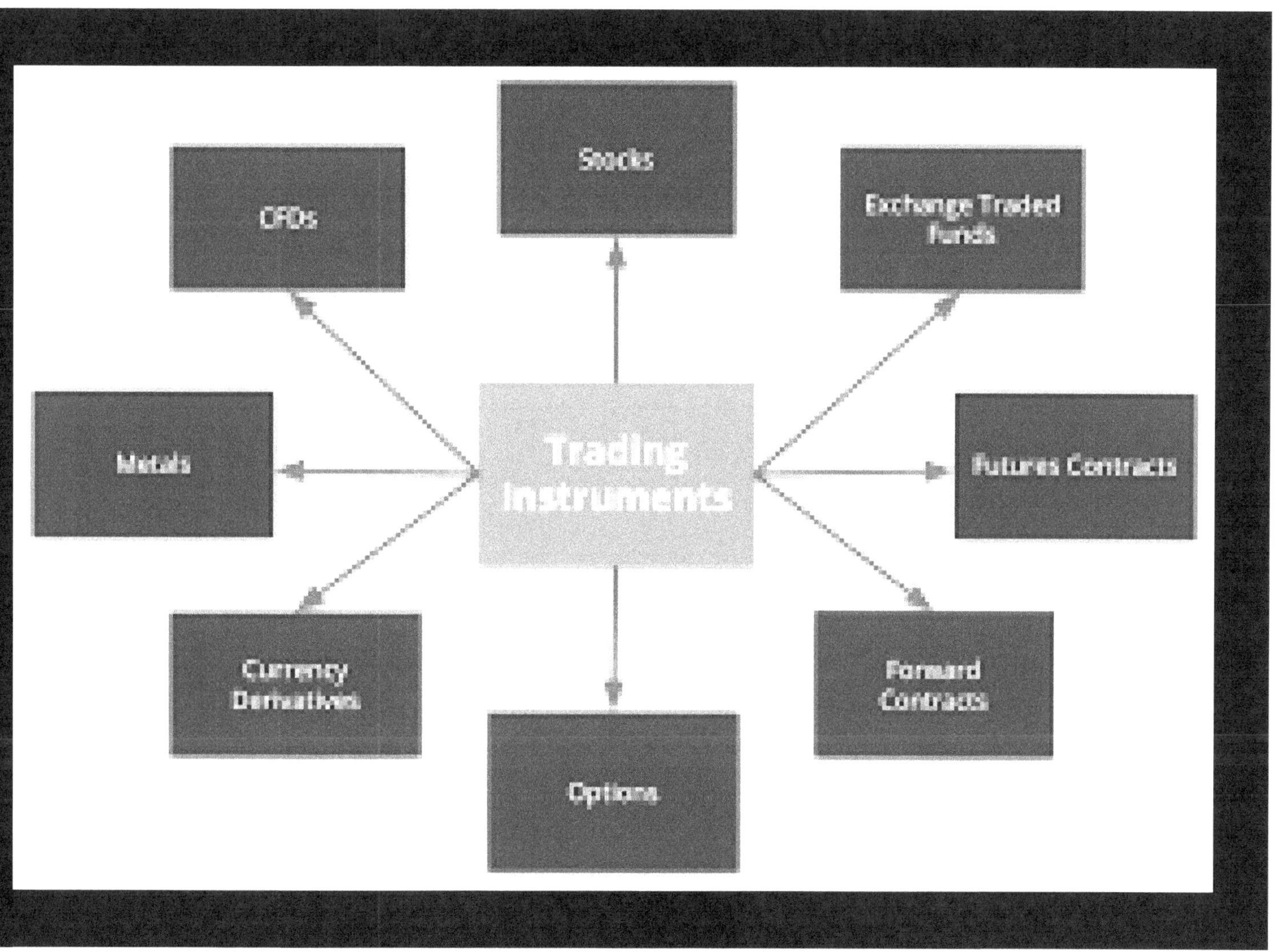

www.ingramcontent.com/pod-product-compliance
Lightning Source LLC
Chambersburg PA
CBHW080249260726
48658CB00008B/3296